I0416409

# PYTHON CODING FOR PROFITABLE FOREX TRADING

## ( 2024 REVISED AND UPDATED EDITION)

**Level Up Your Trading Game: Automate, Analyze, and Profit with Python programming**

**James Vega**

Copyright © 2024 by James Vega. All rights reserved.

No part of this book may be reproduced or transmitted in any form or by any means, electronic or mechanical, including photocopying, recording, or by any information storage and retrieval system, without written permission from the author, except for the inclusion of brief quotations in a review.

## DISCLAIMER

The information contained in this book is provided for informational purposes only and should not be considered as financial advice. The author cannot be held liable for any financial losses or damages incurred by individuals who rely on the information presented in this book.

Trading in the Forex market involves significant risks, and past performance is not necessarily indicative of future results. The author encourages readers to conduct their own research and due diligence before making any trading decisions.

By using this book, you acknowledge and accept the terms of this disclaimer and hold the author harmless from any and all liability arising from your use of the information contained herein.

*To my loving wife, Daniella Vega and my best friend, Paul Simpson, without whose perpetual kicking I would have never accomplished this book*

*And to my baby brother, Christian Vega, who is also making his first steps in the world of data science and Python programming.*

# TABLE OF CONTENT

# PREFACE

Do you dream of financial freedom, of navigating the dynamic world of Forex trading with confidence and purpose? Do you yearn to break free from the shackles of the 9-to-5, to chart your own destiny and unlock wealth potential that traditional investments simply cannot reach?

But let's be honest, the market can seem like a daunting beast, a complex labyrinth guarded by technical jargon and seemingly impenetrable strategies. Fear not, aspiring trader! This book is your key, your decoder ring, your passport to unlocking the secrets of Forex trading and forging your own path to financial independence.

## Who This Book Is For:

☐ The Ambitious Beginner: You're eager to learn, driven to succeed, and possess the hunger to master a new skill. You're ready to step outside your comfort zone and embrace the challenge of the Forex market.

☐ The Frustrated Investor: Tired of meager returns and limited options, you seek more control and potential in your financial future. You're ready to explore new horizons and unlock the power of active trading.

☐ The Tech-Savvy Individual: You embrace technology and understand its potential to revolutionize how we interact with the world. You're excited to leverage the power of Python to simplify and automate your trading journey.

## What This Book Covers:

☐ Demystifying the Forex Market: We break down the jargon, explain key concepts, and equip you with the fundamental knowledge to navigate the market with confidence.

☐ The Power of Python: Forget complex spreadsheets and clunky software. Learn how Python, a powerful and versatile programming language, can streamline your trading and analysis.

☐ Building Winning Strategies: From trend-following to mean reversion, explore diverse trading strategies tailored to your risk tolerance and desired style.

☐ Mastering Order Execution: Take control of your trades with precise order types, time in force options, and advanced execution techniques.

☐ Optimizing Performance: Analyze your results, identify strengths and weaknesses, and refine your strategies for sustainable success.

☐ Navigating the Real World: Understand the emotional challenges, manage risk effectively, and overcome hurdles like slippage and news events.

**To Get the Most Out of This Book:**

☐ Embrace the Hands-On Approach: This book is designed for active learning. Follow the step-by-step guides, experiment with code, and apply your knowledge to simulated and real-world trading.

☐ Don't Be Afraid to Ask Questions: No question is too basic or too complex. Seek clarification, explore online resources, and join communities of fellow traders to expand your knowledge.

☐ Practice Patience and Discipline: Mastering the market takes time and dedication. Be patient with yourself, learn from your mistakes, and remain disciplined in your approach.

Remember, the Journey is the Reward: Enjoy the process of learning, celebrate your victories, and view challenges as opportunities for growth.

This book is your launchpad, your guide on the path to mastering the Forex market. So, strap in, open your mind, and get ready to unlock your inner trading genius!

# Part 1: Introduction to Forex Trading Strategy Development

# Chapter One

## Unveiling the Forex Code – Your Path to Profits

Welcome to the world of Forex trading, where currencies battle for dominance and fortunes are made and lost in the blink of an eye. Aspiring traders may have a sense of being overwhelmed while attempting to navigate this volatile market. Fear not, however!

By the end of this chapter, you will be equipped with the knowledge and tools necessary to unlock the mysteries of the Forex code and pave the way for future riches.

## Transcending the Myths Surrounding Trading Strategies: A World of Options

To have a better understanding of the various trading methods, let's first investigate the landscape of trading strategies. Every strategy comes with its own individual set of potential benefits and drawbacks, making it suitable for a variety of trading styles and levels of risk tolerance.

- Trend-Following: Like riding a wave, this technique capitalizes on known patterns, attempting to purchase when prices rise and sell when they fall. To avoid pursuing transient trends, patience, and discipline are required, even though it has the potential to be rewarding.

- Mean Reversion: Borrowing from the premise that "what goes up, must come down," this approach aims to purchase oversold currencies and sell overbought ones, expecting a return to their average price. However, market trends might linger longer than expected, resulting in possible losses.

- Breakout Trading: Imagine a dam poised to burst - this approach recognizes and capitalizes on occasions when prices break through established support or resistance levels, attempting to capture big price swings. But false breakouts and turbulent markets may lead to huge losses.

- Momentum Trading: Following the "hot hand" mindset, this strategy rides currencies with significant upward momentum, trying to benefit from ongoing gains. However, momentum might wane rapidly, resulting in lost chances or losses if you join in too late.

Each method has its pros and cons, and the optimal way relies on your particular risk tolerance, available time, and market circumstances. Researching and backtesting several strategies helps you select the one that corresponds best with your trading objectives.

## Data-Driven Decisions: Python - Your Secret Weapon

In the fast-paced world of Forex, intuition alone isn't enough. Enter Python, your formidable ally in creating data-driven choices. This flexible programming language reveals a treasure trove of advantages:

- Automation: Eliminate manual processes like data analysis and order execution, freeing up your time for essential decision-making.
- Backtesting: Test your trading techniques using past data to evaluate their performance and uncover possible vulnerabilities before risking actual cash.
- Superior Analysis: Leverage Python's libraries and tools to analyze massive

volumes of market data, identify hidden trends, and provide important insights.

- Customization: Tailor your trading methods to your particular requirements and tastes, giving you an advantage over the competition.

Mastering Python offers you the analytical horsepower to traverse the complexity of the Forex market with confidence.

## Taming the Beast: Market Data, Risks, and Regulations

Remember, the Forex market is a dynamic, breathing beast, ever-evolving and overflowing with intricacies. Here's what you need to know to navigate it safely and effectively:

- Market Data: Understanding diverse data kinds including tick data, order book dynamics, and economic indicators is vital for making educated judgments. Learn how to access, read, and analyze this data using Python.
- Risk Management: Forex trading naturally includes risk. Develop a solid risk management structure that incorporates stop-loss orders, position size tactics, and emotional control to reduce possible losses.
- Rules: Different nations and areas have rules controlling Forex trading. Familiarity with these standards enables you to work inside legal limitations and prevent avoidable hassles.

By understanding the market's complexity and practicing effective risk management, you may approach Forex trading with a calculating attitude, boosting your chances of success.

## Crafting Automated Profits: Building Your Trading App

Now, let's transfer theory into practice. Imagine a sophisticated trading tool, tailored to your tactics and data analysis requirements. a chapter sets the framework for developing an automated profit machine:

- Technical Prerequisites: Understand crucial components including APIs, data connections, and trading platforms to establish the framework for your program.

- App Architecture: Explore several development methodologies and best practices for constructing a modular, efficient, and scalable trading application.
- Integration & Automation: Seamlessly integrate data analysis, strategy execution, and risk management modules into your app, automating essential activities.
- Testing & Refinement: Rigorously test your app utilizing backtesting and simulation methodologies before launching it in the real market.

Remember, your trading software is your customized tool for navigating the Forex market. Invest time in studying its components, refining its features, and extensively evaluating its performance before depending on it for actual transactions.

# Chapter Two

## Python – Your Algorithmic Trading Weapon

In the ever-evolving world of Forex trading, the ability to make rapid, data-driven judgments holds the key to success. This is where Python, your flexible and strong programming language, becomes your algorithmic trading weapon. This chapter digs into Python's particular benefits, allowing you to grasp code, and execution, and harness its potential for successful trades.

## Unleash Python's Power: A Trader's Toolbox

Forget cumbersome spreadsheets and time-consuming manual analysis. Python offers you with a large assortment of advantages for creating effective trading strategies:

- Versatility: From data analysis and visualization to constructing automated trading apps, Python adapts to your different demands.
- Ease of Use: Compared to other programming languages, Python's syntax is comparatively basic and

straightforward, making it accessible for both novices and experienced developers.

- Rich Ecosystem: Explore a huge library of pre-built functions and tools particularly suited for quantitative finance and trading applications.
- Cross-Platform Compatibility: Run your Python code easily across multiple operating systems, guaranteeing flexibility and portability.

Beyond these broad advantages, Python excels in certain areas vital for Forex trading:

- Backtesting & Optimization: Test and develop your tactics using historical data, discovering strengths and shortcomings before risking actual cash.
- Data Mining & Analysis: Analyze massive volumes of market data, revealing

hidden patterns and trends that guide your trading choices.

- Algorithmic Execution: Automate order placement and trade execution, assuring accurate timing and efficient market involvement.

By unleashing the power of Python, you get an advantage in the dynamic world of Forex trading, making data-driven judgments and automating important procedures for possible profit improvement.

## Coding & Execution Made Easy: Mastering the Workflow

Embarking on your Python adventure doesn't need years of coding expertise. Grasping essential principles helps you to travel confidently:

- Memory Management: Understand how Python manages data in memory, optimizing your code for performance and avoiding resource-intensive procedures.

- Interactive Workflows: Leverage Jupyter Notebooks or comparable tools for interactive coding and data exploration, supporting quick development and experimentation.

- Debugging & Troubleshooting: Learn approaches to find and handle faults in your code, ensuring your tactics operate properly.

Remember, regular practice and experimentation are crucial to learning Python's code and execution features. Start with modest projects, gradually add complexity, and don't hesitate to seek advice from online groups and tutorials.

## Connecting the Dots: Integrating with Native Structures

While Python is strong, it doesn't live in a vacuum. Seamless integration with various technology boosts its capabilities:

- Financial APIs: Connect to live market data, trading platforms, and financial service providers, ensuring your strategies have access to real-time information.

- Databases: Integrate Python with databases like MySQL or PostgreSQL to store and handle massive datasets quickly.

- Visualization Tools: Combine Python with tools like Matplotlib or Seaborn to generate bespoke charts and visualizations that illustrate market patterns and insights.

By mastering these integration approaches, you break down boundaries and exploit the capabilities of numerous instruments, producing a streamlined and effective trading environment.

## Testing & Refining: Paper Trading & Backtesting Essentials

Before stepping into the live market, carefully test your methods in a safe environment:

- Paper Trading: Simulate real-world trading with virtual cash, acquiring significant expertise without risking real wealth.
- Backtesting: Evaluate your strategy's effectiveness using historical data, detecting possible vulnerabilities, and

tweaking parameters for superior outcomes.

Testing isn't a one-time occurrence. As market circumstances change and you adjust your techniques, evaluate both paper trading and backtesting to ensure your strategy stays solid and adaptive.

## Live Trading Cautions: Respecting Python's Limitations

While Python is a strong tool, recognizing its limits is vital for prudent trading:

- Performance Bottlenecks: Complex algorithms or inefficient code might lead to performance concerns, possibly hurting live trade executions.

- Data Integrity & Access: Ensure the data you deal with is accurate and dependable, and prevent unauthorized access to critical information.
- Overfitting & Optimization Bias: Be wary of overfitting your techniques to historical data, ensuring they generalize effectively to real-world settings.

By understanding these limits and applying best practices, you guarantee Python acts as a dependable and responsible companion in your trading experience.

# Chapter Three

## Forex Markets from a Developer's Lens: Decoding the Trading Arena

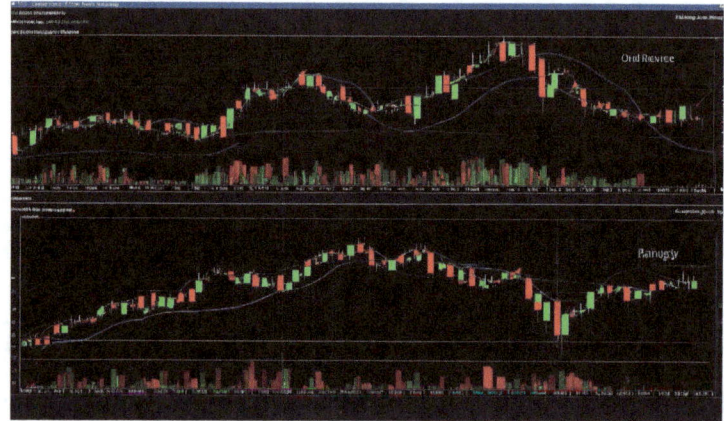

As you commence your Forex trading career, recognizing the playing field is vital. In this chapter, we'll study the complexity of Forex markets via the viewpoint of a developer, arming you with the expertise to traverse these dynamic, digital environments.

# Trading Venues Decoded: A Marketplace of Choices

Imagine a busy marketplace where currencies are continually swapped, values vary in real-time, and billions of dollars transfer hands every day. This, in essence, is the Forex market. But unlike a physical place, it's a decentralized network made up of different trading venues, each with distinct characteristics:

- Interbank Market: The conventional world, accessible exclusively to huge organizations like banks, works electronically but remains mainly opaque.
- Retail Forex Brokers: Cater to individual traders like you, giving a user-friendly interface and access to the interbank market via platforms like MetaTrader.

- Electronic Communication Networks (ECNs): Connect buyers and sellers directly, giving transparency and perhaps narrower spreads.

- Foreign Exchange Matching (FX Matching) Systems: Similar to ECNs but with centralized order matching processes.

Understanding the subtleties of each venue, such as execution speed, liquidity levels, and fee structures, allows you to pick the one that most corresponds with your trading style and objectives.

## Liquidity Secrets: Whales, ECNs, and Aggregation - Know Your Players

Liquidity, the lifeblood of every market, influences how easily you may buy or sell currencies. In Forex, three main actors determine liquidity:

- Whales: Large banks, institutions, and hedge funds with considerable capital, capable of considerably affecting market movements.
- ECNs & FX Matching Systems: By combining orders from numerous players, they generate deeper liquidity pools, possibly delivering narrower spreads.
- Liquidity Providers: These firms give quotations to retail brokers, altering the spreads and order execution accessible to individual traders.

By studying these liquidity actors and their dynamics, you may predict market changes and pick venues with more favorable trading circumstances.

## Instrument Insights: Mastering the Currency Chessboard

The Forex market isn't just about single currencies; it's about pairings traded against one other. Understanding these tools helps you to make educated decisions:

- Major pairings: Highly liquid pairings including EUR/USD, USD/JPY, and GBP/USD, famous for their narrow spreads and volatility.
- Minor Pairs: Combinations of big currencies with less liquidity, possibly enabling increased volatility and specialized trading possibilities.

- Exotic Pairs: Currencies matched with developing markets or fewer traded currencies, incurring more risk and perhaps bigger spreads.

Mastering the features of multiple pairs, together with evaluating economic variables and news events, helps you to locate trading opportunities that fit with your risk tolerance and market expectations.

## Speaking Market Lingo: Decoding the Trading Codex

Like any complicated system, Forex has its language. Demystifying these phrases assists you in comprehending market dynamics and successfully executing trades:

- Pip: The smallest unit of price movement in a currency pair, useful for calculating gains and losses.
- Spread: The difference between the bid (buy) and ask (sell) price, indicates the broker's compensation for facilitating the deal.
- Order Types: Market orders, limit orders, and stop-loss orders — each having a distinct function in entering and leaving transactions.
- Leverage: Borrowing money to multiply prospective earnings (and losses), necessitating careful risk management.
- Technical Analysis & Fundamental Analysis: Two unique ways to study market movements, yielding various insights.

By knowing these important terminology and ideas, you become fluent in the Forex language, navigating market dynamics with confidence and clarity.

# Part 2: Building Your Automated Trading Machine

# Chapter Four

## Deconstructing the Trading App – Your Command Center

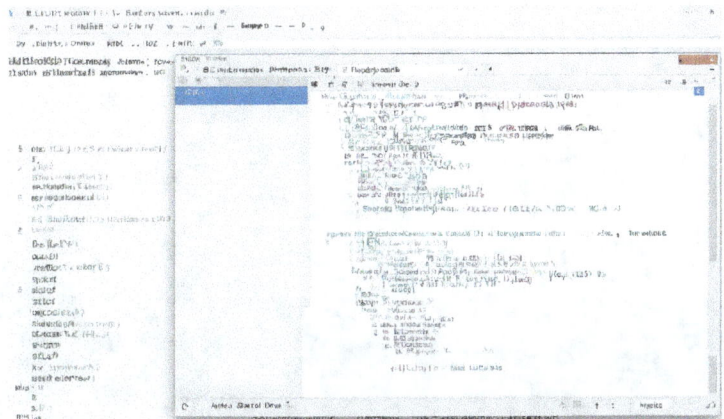

In the fast-paced field of Forex trading, where decisions need to be made in milliseconds, your trading application becomes your critical command center. This chapter looks into the inner workings of these programs, equipping you to grasp their protocols, architecture, and important functions for performing effective transactions.

## Protocol Power: Unveiling the Language of Data Exchange

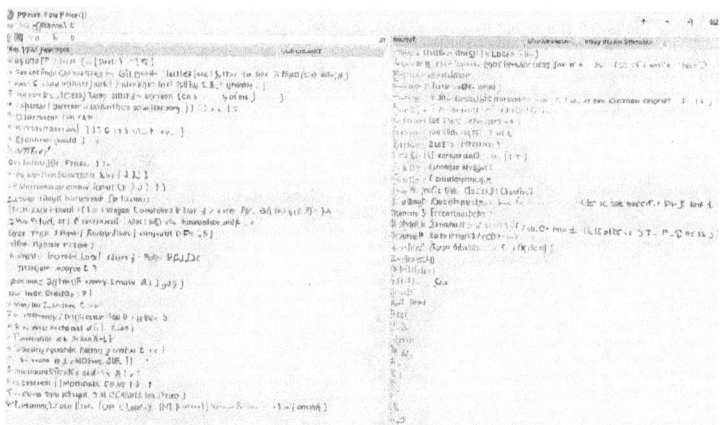

Imagine your trading app as an ambassador, painstakingly speaking with the market on your behalf. This connection depends on specialized protocols, including FIX (Financial Information eXchange), that specify the language for sending orders, getting quotations, and maintaining your account. Understanding these protocols helps you to:

- Optimize communication: Ensure smooth and efficient data sharing between your app and the market, eliminating delays and improving execution speed.
- Troubleshoot issues: Identify and repair any communication faults that might impair your trading activity.
- Choose the correct tools: Select trading platforms and programs that support the protocols relevant to your selected market and broker.

Remember, a good grasp of communication protocols creates the basis for an effective and trustworthy connection with the market.

## Layers Unraraveling: Exploring the App's Inner Workings

Think of your trading app as a tiered cake, each piece having a particular purpose:

- Presentation Layer: The user interface where you interact with the program, placing orders, monitoring locations, and evaluating data.

- Business Logic Layer: The brains of the operation, where trading strategies are performed, orders are issued, and risk management regulations are enforced.

- Data Access Layer: Connects to numerous data sources, obtaining market quotations, historical data, and account information.

- Communication Layer: Handles data interchange with the market using protocols like FIX, providing smooth interaction.

By knowing these layers and their roles, you can grasp the intricacy of your trading software and its involvement in executing your trading methods.

## Risk Management Arsenal: Protecting Your Capital, Minimizing Losses

Forex trading naturally includes risk. This is when your trading app's risk management arsenal comes into play:

- Stop-loss orders: Automatically abandon transactions when prices hit a specified threshold, reducing possible losses.
- Take-profit orders: Automatically lock in profits when prices hit a specified level.

- Position sizing: Allocate a specified amount of your cash to each transaction, limiting overexposure and catastrophic losses.
- Trailing stop-loss: Dynamically alter stop-loss levels as prices move positively, safeguarding profits while allowing for additional gains.

By implementing these sophisticated risk management tools into your trading software and following basic risk management principles, you navigate the market with better discipline and safeguard your cash from large losses.

## Order Precision: Crafting Clarity in Execution

When ordering orders, accuracy is key. Your trading software enables you to set multiple order types to execute your plans optimally:

- Market orders: Executed instantly at the best available market price.
- Limit orders: Executed just when the price hits your set limit, assuring you purchase cheap or sell high.
- Stop-loss orders: As indicated previously, automatically quit trades at a specified price to minimize losses.
- Time-in-force orders: Specify the period your order is valid, eliminating lost opportunities or unintentional executions.

Mastering these order types helps you to create accurate execution plans matched with your market expectations and risk tolerance.

## Beyond the Basics: Advanced App Features

While the main operations outlined above are vital, discover advanced features for increased trading capabilities:

- Backtesting and optimization: Test your tactics using historical data inside your app, improving them before risking actual cash.
- Algorithmic trading: Automate complicated trading techniques, freeing up your time for analysis and decision-making.

- Customizable dashboards: Tailor your app's UI to present the information most relevant to your trading style and approach.

Remember, researching and understanding these advanced features may considerably enhance your trading experience and perhaps increase your outcomes.

# Chapter Five

## Data Mastery with Python – Fueling Your Strategies

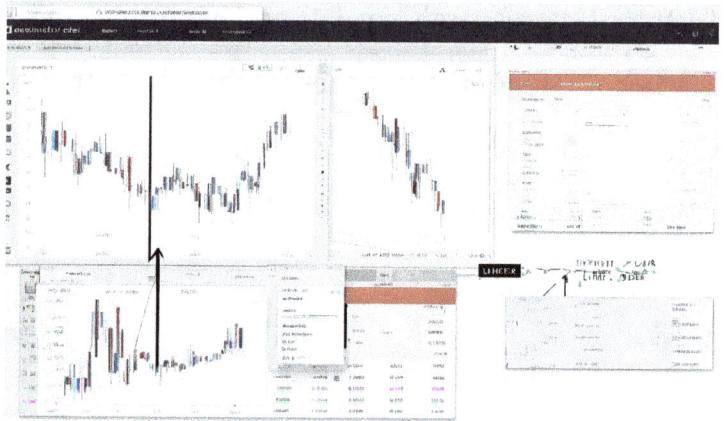

In the dynamic world of Forex trading, where choices rest on transient patterns and tiny adjustments, data reigns supreme. This chapter digs into the art of harvesting market data using Python, helping you to feed your strategies with useful insights and maximize your trading success.

## Tick by Tick: Demystifying the Data Flow

Imagine the market as a river, always flowing with information. Each "tick" is a single data point, collecting the price, volume, and timestamp of every transaction, order, and quotation change. Understanding these ticks is critical for:

- Market Analysis: Analyze historical tick data to detect repeating trends, analyze volatility, and backtest your ideas for efficacy.
- Strategy Refinement: Refine your entry and exit criteria based on tick-level

analysis, aiming for higher accuracy and possible profit maximization.

- Live Trading Decisions: Utilize real-time tick data to respond to rapid market fluctuations and make trades depending on live circumstances.

By comprehending the notion of ticks and timestamps, you open a deeper knowledge of market dynamics and pave the road for data-driven decision-making.

## Order Book Dynamics: Decoding the Hidden Market Pulse

Beyond individual deals, the order book exposes the aggregate intentions of market players. This secret treasure, continually updated with purchase and sell orders at various prices, provides vital insights:

- Market Depth: Analyze the amount of orders at various price levels to determine probable support and resistance regions.
- Order Imbalance: Identify buy or sell order dominance, possibly anticipating future price fluctuations.
- Liquidity Assessment: Evaluate the available liquidity at your targeted price point, guaranteeing seamless order execution.

By learning to access and analyze order book data using Python, you get a significant advantage in analyzing market sentiment and finding prospective trading opportunities.

## Data Compression & Retrieval: Optimizing for Speed and Efficiency

Raw market data is enormous, and processing it properly is vital. This is where Python's data compression and retrieval algorithms come into play:

- Compression Techniques: Reduce data size without compromising vital information, lowering storage needs and transmission times.
- Efficient Retrieval Libraries: Leverage libraries like Pandas and NumPy to load, filter, and manipulate massive datasets quickly and effectively.
- Caching Mechanisms: Store frequently requested data locally, avoiding duplicate

queries and optimizing processing performance.

By improving your data handling pipelines using Python, you guarantee your strategies have access to timely and relevant information, allowing agile decision-making in the fast-paced trading market.

## Universal Data Connector: Bridging Live and Saved Data Seamlessly

Your trading path entails examining both historical and present data. Python libraries like "OandaAPI" or "ccxt" bridge this gap by:

- Connecting to Live Data Feeds: Stream real-time market data straight into your Python environment, allowing you to respond to live market moves.

- Accessing Historical Data: Download historical data from numerous sources, enabling you to backtest your strategy and study prior market movements.

- Streamlining Data Integration: Standardize data formats and structures, simplifying analysis and removing needless conversion procedures.

This seamless integration of current and historical data allows you to design strategies that respond to altering market circumstances while harnessing useful lessons from prior success.

# Beyond the Basics: Advanced Data Techniques

As your understanding improves, investigate advanced data management methods for deeper insights:

- Machine Learning & AI: Train computers to spot patterns and make predictions, perhaps finding hidden possibilities.
- Sentiment Analysis: Analyze news and social media data to measure market sentiment and probable price moves.
- High-Frequency Trading (HFT): Develop techniques that profit on transient market inefficiencies, requiring substantial expertise and risk management measures.

# Chapter Six

## Beyond Technicals - Unveiling Fundamental Analysis

While technical analysis focuses on price charts and indicators, a comprehensive approach to Forex trading necessitates studying the underlying reasons that drive market movements: fundamental analysis. This chapter digs into economic impacts, political events, and industry-specific insights, helping you to make educated choices based on a better grasp of the market environment.

## Economic Insights: Decoding the News Cycle

Imagine the global economy as a complicated interaction of elements including interest rates, inflation, GDP growth, and unemployment. Changes in key economic data strongly affect currency values. By knowing these connections, you can:

- Predict future trends: Analyze impending economic releases like central bank interest rate decisions or inflation data to forecast their influence on certain currency pairings.
- Identify trading opportunities: Capitalize on market responses to economic news, possibly earning from short-term price changes.

- Assess long-term market direction: Integrate economic fundamentals into your trading approach, getting a greater grasp of probable long-term trends.

Remember, economic data releases may generate substantial volatility. Employing appropriate risk management tactics is vital during these moments.

## Political Savvy: Understanding the World Stage

Politics and economy are interwoven. Elections, policy changes, and geopolitical concerns may substantially impact currency prices. By remaining informed, you can:

- Anticipate prospective events: Monitor impending elections, policy debates, and potential geopolitical flashpoints to analyze their influence on certain currencies.
- Identify risk factors: Understand how political instability or trade disputes may heighten volatility and possibly damage your trading holdings.
- Adapt your strategies: Adjust your trading technique depending on altering political landscapes, limiting possible losses, and optimizing profit prospects.

Remember, remaining politically educated doesn't entail becoming a political pundit. Focus on events and policies having proven influence on the markets you trade.

## Industry–Specific Events: Unveiling Hidden Gems

Beyond broad economic and political reasons, industry-specific events may also impact currency pairings. For example, news concerning oil prices might affect the value of oil-exporting nations' currencies. By grasping these subtleties, you can:

- Identify niche possibilities: Focus on particular sectors related to your selected currency pairings, revealing unique trading chances.
- acquire deeper insights: Analyze industry-specific reports and statistics to acquire a more thorough knowledge of possible pricing fluctuations.

- Diversify your strategies: Integrate industry-specific knowledge into your larger trading technique, lowering risk and perhaps boosting profits.

Remember, specializing in certain sectors demands in-depth study and a deep comprehension of their dynamics. Start by concentrating on sectors closely connected to the currency pairs you trade most often.

## The Balanced Approach: Integrating Fundamentals with Technicals

Technical and fundamental analysis give diverse viewpoints. Combining these gives a well-rounded approach to trading:

- Technical analysis gives entry and exit signals: Identify prospective trading opportunities based on chart patterns and indicators.
- Fundamental analysis validates and contextualizes: Validate technical signals by understanding the underlying economic, political, and industry-specific variables impacting price changes.
- Risk management becomes refined: Use fundamental research to determine larger market risks and modify your position size and stop-loss levels appropriately.

Remember, there's no one-size-fits-all method. Experiment and discover the balance that corresponds with your trading style, risk tolerance, and favorite information sources.

## Beyond the Basics: Advanced Fundamental Analysis Techniques

As you develop, consider further approaches to enhance your basic analysis:

- Econometric Modeling: Analyze complicated economic interactions using statistical models to anticipate future developments and their influence on particular currencies.
- Sentiment Analysis: Gauge market sentiment by evaluating news stories, social media data, and investor surveys to detect prospective movements in demand and supply.
- Fundamental movement Analysis: Track the movement of money into and out of

various economies to evaluate probable future currency values.

Remember, these sophisticated procedures demand substantial expertise and money. Start by learning the basic concepts of fundamental analysis before entering into more difficult regions.

# Chapter Seven

## Technical Analysis - Turning Indicators into Python Code

### Demystifying Market Language

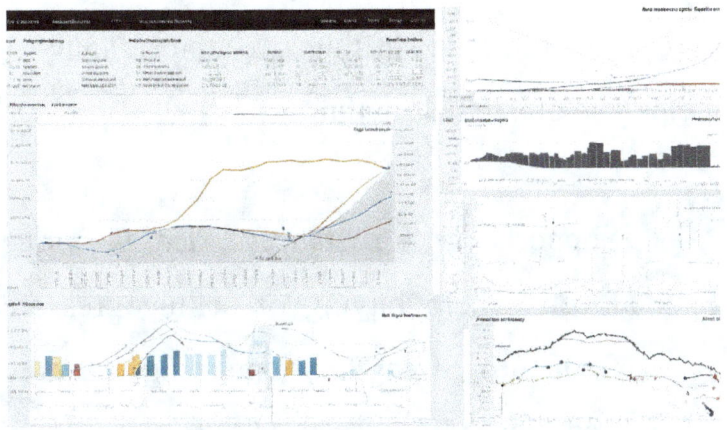

While fundamental research digs into the "why" underlying market moves, technical analysis focuses on the "how," reading price charts and indicators to uncover trading opportunities. This chapter equips you to leverage the power of technical analysis and convert common indicators into Python code, translating market signals into actionable insights.

## Market Velocity & Filters: Deciphering the Chart's Rhythm

Imagine the market as a dynamic dance, with prices continually shifting. Technical analysis helps you grasp this rhythm:

- Support & Resistance: Identify price levels where buying or selling pressure frequently strengthens, pointing at future trend reversals or continuations.
- Trend Analysis: Define the general price direction (uptrend, downtrend, or sideways) to influence your entry and exit points.

- Market Velocity: Analyze the pace and severity of price changes using indicators like Average True Range (ATR) to determine volatility and risk potential.

By grasping these ideas, you set the framework for utilizing numerous technical indications efficiently.

## Coding TA Indicators: Python Powers Your Analysis Arsenal

Now, let's put theory into practice. This chapter leads you through writing common technical indicators using Python:

- Moving Averages: Smooth price data and discover patterns by computing the average price for a specified time. Explore Simple Moving Average (SMA),

Exponential Moving Average (EMA), and Weighted Moving Average (WMA) variants.

- Relative Strength Index (RSI): Gauge overbought and oversold situations by evaluating recent market movements. Learn to code both traditional and stochastic RSI for more nuanced insights.
- Bollinger Bands: Define support and resistance zones based on volatility, suggesting possible breakout or breakdown chances. Implement upper and lower bands dynamically depending on standard deviations.

Remember, each indication has its strengths and drawbacks. Experiment with multiple indicators and coding modifications to discover the ones that best fit your trading style and preferences.

# Visualizing Insights: Charting Your Path to Success

Data visualization plays a key part in technical analysis:

- Interactive Charts: Use tools like Matplotlib or Plotly to build interactive charts, dynamically altering indicators and settings for deeper study.
- Customizable Overlays: Visualize numerous indicators on the same chart, facilitating pattern detection and identification of trade signals.
- Heatmaps & Correlation Matrices: Explore connections between various currencies or indices using heatmaps or correlation matrices, finding possible diversification possibilities.

By mastering data visualization, you convert raw data into captivating tales that drive your trading choices and increase your entire trading experience.

## Beyond the Basics: Advanced Technical Analysis Techniques

As you develop, investigate advanced approaches for even deeper insights:

- Elliott Wave Theory: Identify recurrent price patterns that imply future trend continuations or reversals.
- Fibonacci Retracements & Extensions: Predict possible support and resistance levels based on past price movements.

- Harmonics & Price Patterns: Analyze certain chart patterns to uncover high-probability trading opportunities.

Remember, these sophisticated approaches need a firm basis in fundamental technical analysis and a complete comprehension of their underlying concepts.

# Chapter Eight

## Visualizing Forex Markets – Painting a Winning Picture

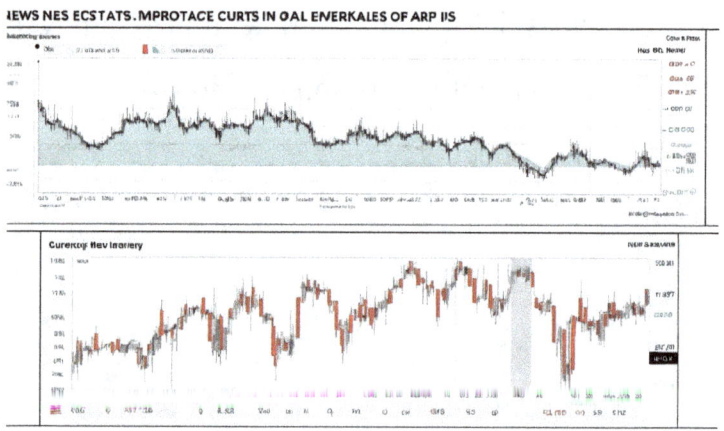

In the fast-paced world of Forex trading, information overload may impair smart decision-making. This chapter digs into the art of data visualization, equipping you to translate market data into clear, actionable insights using Python's sophisticated charting packages.

By constructing a "winning picture" of market dynamics, you get a critical advantage in detecting trading opportunities and enhancing your techniques.

## Charting Essentials: Mastering the Brushstrokes

Imagine making a complex artwork; data visualization takes comparable brushstrokes. Before getting into sophisticated charts, grasp the fundamentals:

- Matplotlib & Pandas: Embrace these vital libraries - Matplotlib for flexible charting and Pandas for data processing.
- Line Plots & Scatter Plots: Understand these fundamental plot patterns to

visualize price changes, correlations, and trendlines.

- Candlestick & OHLC Charts: Dive deeper with candlestick charts illustrating open, high, low, and closing prices for each period.

By learning these core charting methods, you build the foundations for generating useful and insightful visualizations.

## Live & Static Data Visualization: Capturing the Market Dance

Markets never sleep, and so should your visions. Explore techniques for presenting both current and historical data:

- Live Streaming Charts: Use libraries like "fxcmpy" to stream real-time market data into your charts, viewing dynamic price moves as they happen.

- Interactive Charts: Employ libraries like "Plotly" to generate interactive charts, enabling you to zoom, pan, and alter settings for deeper analysis on the fly.

- Historical Data Exploration: Visualize historical data from many sources using Pandas for complete trend analysis and backtesting applications.

Remember, the selected visualization approach relies on your unique demands. Live streaming allows real-time decision-making, while historical investigation assists in strategy refining and analyzing long-term patterns.

## Chart Enhancements: Adding Depth and Color to Your Masterpiece

Beyond basic plots, modify your charts for greater analysis:

- Overlays & Technical Indicators: Overlay several indicators like moving averages, RSI, or Bollinger Bands on your charts for easy pattern detection and signal identification.

- Volume Bars & Histograms: Visualize trade volume with price changes to judge market mood and possible breakouts.

- Annotations & Drawings: Add trendlines, support/resistance lines, and text annotations to emphasize significant chart aspects and express your trading ideas graphically.

By creatively applying these additions, you convert your charts from static data representations into appealing tales that lead your trading choices with clarity and confidence.

## Beyond the Basics: Advanced Visualization Techniques

As your skill increases, try advanced approaches for even deeper insights:

- Heatmaps & Correlation Matrices: Visualize links between multiple currencies or indices using heatmaps or correlation matrices, uncovering possible diversification possibilities or hidden hazards.

- 3D Plotting: Utilize libraries like "Mayavi" for 3D visualizations, examining complicated information from numerous perspectives and revealing hidden patterns.
- Custom Charting Libraries: Explore specialist libraries like "TA-Lib" or "yfinance" for pre-built technical indicators and sophisticated charting features.

Remember, advancing into advanced procedures demands a deep grasp of the underlying concepts and your data's unique requirements. Start by understanding the main visualization approaches before investigating these specific tools.

# Part 3: Strategies, Execution, and Evaluating Success

# Chapter Nine

## Cracking the Strategy Code – Alpha & Beta Explained

### Demystifying Performance and Building Winning Approaches

In the competitive realm of Forex trading, deciphering the ocean of information and building sustainable strategy demands a thorough dive into performance factors and successful tactics.

This chapter digs into the ideas of alpha and beta, discusses conventional trading methods, and examines the promise and limitations of market creation and high-frequency trading (HFT) using Python.

## Performance Pillars: Alpha & Beta – Unveiling the Hidden Engines

Imagine two traders: Mark constantly exceeds the market, while Sarah follows it closely. What's the difference? The solution resides in alpha and beta:

- Alpha: Represents the extra return created by a strategy relative to the market benchmark (like a market index). It demonstrates talent and unique ideas that exceed the "average."

- Beta: Measures the volatility of a strategy compared to the market. A greater beta predicts wider fluctuations in returns, both positive and negative.

Understanding these principles permits you to:

- Evaluate strategy performance: Analyze alpha and beta to find strategies with consistent excess returns and control risk related to their volatility.
- Optimize your portfolio: Combine strategies with varying alphas and betas to create desired risk-return profiles and diversify your holdings.

Remember, alpha creation is tough and involves ongoing learning, adaptability, and a thorough grasp of market dynamics.

## Classic Strategies Demystified: Your Trading Arsenal Explained

Beyond knowing performance determinants, learning traditional methods qualifies you for numerous market conditions:

- Trend-Following: Capitalize on known trends by purchasing rising assets and selling falling ones, utilizing indicators like moving averages or trendlines.
- Mean Reversion: Exploit transient departures from an asset's average price by purchasing inexpensive assets and

selling overpriced ones, utilizing tools like Bollinger Bands or RSI.

- Breakout: Identify and capitalize on probable price breakouts above resistance levels or below support levels, utilizing chart patterns or volatility indicators.

- Momentum: Ride significant market swings in either direction by purchasing assets with growing momentum and selling those with diminishing momentum, utilizing indicators like MACD or Stochastic Oscillator.

- By understanding these key methods and adjusting them to your risk tolerance and market insights, you develop a diverse trading toolkit.

# Market Making & HFT with Python: Understanding the Complexities

While Python enables different trading tactics, moving into market making and HFT demands considerable skill and resources:

- Market Making: Providing constant buy and sell quotations for particular assets, requiring extensive liquidity management, complicated algorithms, and high-frequency execution capabilities.

- HFT: Exploiting ephemeral market inefficiencies via quick order execution and complex algorithms, necessitating expert programming skills, deep market knowledge, and major infrastructure investment.

Remember, both market making and HFT entail substantial risks and are not recommended for novices. A thorough study, knowing the potential hazards, and holding the appropriate resources are vital before delving into these areas.

## Beyond the Basics: Exploring Advanced Strategies and Techniques

As your knowledge and expertise improve, try researching advanced strategies:

- Algorithmic Trading: Automate trading choices based on predetermined rules and technical analysis, allowing for quicker execution and perhaps smoother returns.
- Statistical Arbitrage: Exploit price disparities across multiple marketplaces or

instruments using complicated statistical models.

- Machine Learning & AI: Train computers to spot patterns and make predictions, perhaps finding hidden possibilities.

Remember, each advanced approach has its intricacies and demands a complete grasp of its possible advantages and hazards. Start by understanding the foundations and proceed progressively, focusing on sensible risk management along your path.

# Chapter Ten

## Order Mastery & Simulations – Executing with Confidence

In the fast-paced world of Forex trading, flawless execution is crucial. This chapter looks into the nuances of order types, time-in-force choices, and the power of simulations, equipping you to execute your strategy with confidence and reduce execution risks.

## Order Types Explained: Unlocking Your Trading Arsenal

Imagine your instructions as your trade army, with each soldier having a distinct role:

- Market Orders: Executed instantly at the best available market price, useful for catching rapid chances but lacking accuracy.

- Limit Orders: Executed only when the price hits your set limit, assuring you purchase cheap or sell high but possibly missing ephemeral possibilities.

- Stop Orders: Protect your holdings by automatically leaving trades when the price hits a specified threshold, limiting possible losses.

- Stop-Loss Orders: A special sort of stop order, automatically terminating transactions at a preset loss level, vital for risk management.

- Take-Profit Orders: Automatically lock in profits when the price hits your targeted level, securing gains and avoiding emotional-based judgments.

- Trailing Stop-Loss Orders: Dynamically alter stop-loss levels as prices move positively, safeguarding gains while allowing for greater gain potential.

- Compound Orders: Combine numerous order types into a single execution, allowing complicated techniques like OCO (One Cancels the Other) or bracket orders.

Mastering these order types helps you to execute your ideas exactly, adjust to changing market circumstances, and manage risk efficiently.

# Time in Force: Defining the Order's Lifespan

Imagine giving your trading orders an expiry date. Time in force choices influence how long your orders stay valid:

- GTC (Good-Til-Canceled): The order stays active until manually canceled or filled, useful for long-term plans.
- GTD (Good-Til-Date): The order stays active until a certain date, useful for expiring options or special market occurrences.
- GTT (Good-Til-Time): The order stays active until a certain time, helpful for intraday trading sessions.
- IOC (Immediate-or-Cancel): Filled instantly or canceled, assuring execution

at the present price but perhaps missing partial fills.

- FOK (Fill-or-Kill): Filled or canceled promptly, assuring full execution or avoiding partial fills.

Understanding these time-in-force choices helps you modify your orders to meet your desired execution timeline and prevent unwanted outcomes.

## Simulating Success: Testing Your Strategies in a Safe Sandbox

Before moving into actual trading, simulators provide a vital testing ground:

- Historical Data: Backtest your strategies using historical data to judge their performance under various market situations.

- Paper Trading: Execute simulated trades with virtual money, building expertise and confidence without risking real wealth.
- Forward Testing: Test your tactics on live data in a virtual environment, replicating real-world execution and spotting any flaws.

By introducing simulations into your trading process, you:

- Refine your strategies: Identify and resolve any vulnerabilities before risking actual wealth.
- Manage emotions: Gain experience making trading choices in a simulated

setting, lowering possible emotional impacts on actual transactions.

- Build confidence: Develop a comfort level with your selected strategy and execution tools before going live.

Remember, simulations are great tools, but real-world markets might vary. Use them as a learning opportunity, not a guarantee of future success.

## Beyond the Basics: Advanced Order Management Techniques

As your experience increases, investigate advanced order management techniques:

- Algo Trading: Automate order execution based on specified rules and technical analysis, providing quicker response times and perhaps smoother returns.

- Dark Pools & OTC Trading: Participate in alternative trading platforms with less transparency, demanding extensive expertise and large cash.
- Portfolio Rebalancing: Maintain your intended asset allocation by automatically altering holdings depending on market fluctuations.

Delving into advanced procedures takes substantial knowledge, expertise, and risk management best practices. Start by grasping the main order types and execution techniques before investigating these difficult topics.

# Chapter Eleven

## Backtesting & Performance Analysis - Theory Meets Reality: Unveiling the Hidden Truths

The appeal of every trading technique rests in its potential performance. This chapter digs into the art of backtesting and performance analysis using Python, equipping you to translate theoretical concepts into measurable facts and analyze their feasibility in the real world.

By bridging the gap between theory and reality, you obtain vital insights to develop your methods and maximize your trading trip.

## Modular App Architecture: Building for Speed and Efficiency

Imagine backtesting as a complicated machine; its design defines its processing power. Consider these fundamental principles:

- Modular Design: Break down your backtesting program into discrete modules focused on data loading, strategy logic, and performance analysis. This enhances code reusability, and maintainability, and simplifies future upgrades.

- Parallel Processing: Harness the power of multithreading to examine multiple market periods concurrently, dramatically lowering backtesting time and allowing bigger data sets. Libraries like "multiprocessing" or "concurrent. futures" facilitate parallel execution.

- Caching Mechanisms: Store frequently accessible data like past prices locally, eliminating duplicate queries and speeding processing performance. Libraries like "joblib" provide effective caching methods.

By architecting your backtesting application properly, you guarantee it can perform complicated analyses rapidly, permitting you to investigate multiple situations and modify your tactics with agility.

## Multithreading Power: Unleashing the Parallel Processing Potential

Imagine studying numerous years of historical data consecutively; backtesting may become time-consuming. Multithreading gives a solution:

- Concurrent Strategy Execution: Divide your backtesting process into smaller jobs (e.g., evaluating particular months) and run them concurrently on various cores. This considerably decreases overall processing time.
- Efficient Resource Use: Optimize hardware use by spreading backtesting workloads across available CPU cores, maximizing processing capability.
- Dynamic Thread Management: Adjust the number of threads depending on your hardware capabilities and data size to provide optimum performance without overloading your system.

Remember, although multithreading delivers great performance improvements, it adds complexity. Start by learning single-threaded backtesting before diving into this sophisticated approach.

## Analyzing Results: Decoding the Secrets of Equity Curves and Statistics

Backtesting outcomes go beyond basic wins and losses. Understanding essential performance measures is crucial:

- Equity Curve: Visualize the cumulative performance of your strategy over time, noting times of growth, drawdown, and possible risk regions.

- Sharpe Ratio: Measure the risk-adjusted return of your approach, comparing its profitability to the degree of risk involved.

- Sortino Ratio: Similar to the Sharpe ratio but penalizes just downside deviations, offering a better view of downside risk.

- Maximum Drawdown: Identify the biggest peak-to-trough decrease in your strategy's equity curve, showing probable maximum losses.

- Win Rate & Profit Factor: Analyze the proportion of winning trades and the average profit relative to average loss, offering insights into trading frequency and overall profitability.

By assessing these indicators in combination with your selected timeframes and market circumstances, you receive vital insights into your strategy's strengths, shortcomings, and possibilities for real-world applicability.

## Beyond the Basics: Advanced Backtesting & Optimization Techniques

As your expertise increases, try further approaches for deeper analysis:

- Monte Carlo Simulations: Run your strategy through several random market scenarios to examine its resilience and potential performance under varied situations.

- Parameter Optimization: Optimize strategy parameters using tools like "Scikit-optimize" to identify the combination that optimizes possible returns or reduces risk.

- Machine Learning Integration: Train algorithms to uncover lucrative trends in historical data and integrate these insights into your backtesting and strategy formulation.

Remember, these sophisticated strategies demand a firm foundation in backtesting foundations and a deep comprehension of their underlying intricacies. Start by understanding the key analytical measures and progressively proceed towards more advanced methodologies.

Remember, backtesting is not a guarantee of future success, but an important step in evaluating the strengths and flaws of your technique before moving into real trading.

Continuous learning, proper risk management, and continual review are crucial to navigating the changing world of Forex trading with confidence and a data-driven perspective.

# Part 4: From Strategy to Live Trading & Beyond

# Chapter Twelve

## From Code to Profits – Implementing Your First Strategy: Unleashing the Power of Python

With the information gathered from earlier chapters, you're now set to put theory into practice. This chapter leads you through building your first Forex trading strategy using Python, concentrating on a traditional Trend-Following method.

By converting principles into actual code, you acquire hands-on experience, develop confidence, and take your first step toward navigating the fascinating world of live trading.

# Trend-Following in Action: Demystifying the Strategy

Imagine surfing the waves of market trends; Trend-Following capitalizes on this principle:

- Identify Trends: Use technical indicators like Moving Averages or ADX to identify established trends (upward or downward).
- Enter Trades: Enter positions by the recognized trend (buy for uptrends, sell for downtrends) using precise entry criteria.
- Exit Trades: Manage positions and safeguard profits using established exit criteria based on technical indicators, trailing stops, or timeframes.

This strategy seeks to capture persistent price movements while reducing losses during possible reversals.

## Building Your Strategy Code – Step-by-Step Guide

Let's transfer theory into action:

- Data Acquisition: Use libraries like "fxcmpy" or "yfinance" to obtain historical pricing data for your selected currency pair.
- Trend Identification: Implement selected technical indicators (e.g., Moving Averages) using libraries like "pandas-ta" or "ta-lib" to detect trend directions.
- Entry Rules: Define unambiguous entry criteria based on trend confirmation and

other indicators like RSI or Stochastic Oscillator.

- Exit Rules: Establish exit strategies employing trailing stop-losses, set profit objectives, or time-based exits to minimize risk and safeguard gains.

- Position Sizing: Implement solid money management concepts, using approaches like the 1% rule or Kelly Criterion to identify acceptable trade sizes depending on your account balance and risk tolerance.

- Backtesting & Optimization: Thoroughly backtest your strategy using historical data, studying performance indicators including equity curve, Sharpe ratio, and maximum drawdown. Refine entry, exit, and money management rules depending on backtesting outcomes.

Remember, this is a simple foundation. Explore more indicators, change rules, and backtest extensively to adjust the approach to your tastes and risk tolerance.

## Money Management Essentials: Safeguarding Your Capital

In the unpredictable world of Forex, risk management is paramount:

- Position Sizing: Limit the risk of each transaction to a modest proportion of your account balance (e.g., 1-2%).
- Stop-Loss Orders: Always use stop-loss orders to automatically exit losing trades and reduce possible losses.

- Risk-Reward Ratio: Ensure your potential earnings surpass possible losses by aiming for a 2:1 or higher risk-reward ratio.
- Diversification: Spread your wealth over several currency pairings and techniques to lessen the effect of individual losses.
- Emotional Control: Avoid hasty actions influenced by fear or greed; adhere to your stated rules and trading strategy.

By adopting basic money management practices, you develop a basis for sustainable trading and handle market volatility with more confidence.

## Beyond the Basics: Exploring Advanced Strategies and Techniques

As your expertise and experience increase, try studying advanced approaches:

- Multi-Timeframe Analysis: Combine analysis on several timescales to find long-term trends and short-term entry/exit chances.
- Mean Reversion methods: Combine Trend-Following with Mean Reversion methods to catch both trending and reversing market movements.
- Algorithmic Trading: Automate your trading based on specified rules and indications, allowing quicker execution and perhaps smoother returns.

Remember, delving into sophisticated procedures demands a full awareness of their intricacies and possible hazards. Prioritize mastering the core fundamentals and practice responsible risk management before exploring these advanced domains.

# Chapter Thirteen

## Evaluating Performance - Beyond Wins & Losses: Unveiling the Nuances and Optimizing Your Journey

Congratulations, you've applied your first strategy and joined the dynamic world of live trading! While chasing profits is enticing, truly successful traders know it's about sustainable performance and continuous improvement. This chapter delves into performance evaluation beyond wins and losses, empowering you to analyze your trades objectively, understand leverage risks, and optimize your strategies responsibly.

# Performance Metrics Unveiled: Unmasking the Hidden Truths

Wins and losses tell only part of the story. Analyze your performance with key metrics:

- Return on Equity (ROE): Measures overall profitability relative to your starting capital.
- Profit Factor: Compares average winning trade size to average losing trade size, indicating trading efficiency.
- Sharpe Ratio: Balances profitability with risk, a higher ratio implying better risk-adjusted returns.
- Sortino Ratio: Similar to Sharpe but penalizes only downside deviations, providing a clearer picture of downside risk.

- Maximum Drawdown: Identifies the largest peak-to-trough decline, highlighting potential worst-case scenarios.
- Transaction Costs: Consider commissions, spreads, and other fees impacting your net returns.

By analyzing these metrics alongside your trading logs, you gain valuable insights into your strategy's strengths, weaknesses, and potential areas for improvement.

## Leverage Explained: Amplifying Gains (and Losses):

Leverage allows you to control larger positions with less capital, potentially amplifying profits.

However, misusing leverage can also magnify losses significantly.

- Understand Leverage Ratios: Know how much leverage you're using and its impact on potential gains and losses.
- Manage Risk Strictly: Employ strict stop-loss orders and limit margin utilization to mitigate potential losses from adverse market movements.
- Start Small & Gradually Increase: Begin with low leverage and gradually increase only as you gain experience and confidence in risk management.

Remember, leverage is a powerful tool, not a shortcut to riches. Use it responsibly and prioritize capital preservation over chasing unrealistic gains.

# Optimizing Strategies: Walking the Fine Line Between Improvement and Overfitting

As you analyze your performance, you'll naturally seek improvements. However, be wary of overfitting:

- Backtesting Overfitting: When your strategy performs exceptionally well in backtesting but poorly in live trading, it might be "overfitted" to specific historical data.

- Parameter Overfitting: Adjusting strategy parameters excessively based on limited data can lead to misleading performance and potential failure in real-world scenarios.

- Focus on Robust Strategies: Aim for strategies with consistent performance across diverse market conditions, not just specific historical periods.

- Prioritize Simplicity: Complex strategies might appear "better" in backtests but can be prone to overfitting and harder to manage in reality.

- Out-of-Sample Testing: Evaluate your strategy on data not used in backtesting to assess its generalizability and avoid overfitting.

Remember, optimization is an ongoing process. Experiment judiciously, prioritize generalizability, and avoid the temptations of overfitting to ensure your strategies can translate theory into sustainable real-world profits.

## Beyond the Basics: Advanced Performance Analysis Techniques

As your expertise grows, explore advanced techniques:

- Monte Carlo Simulations: Analyze your strategy's performance under various random market scenarios to assess its robustness and potential performance under diverse conditions.
- Machine Learning Integration: Train algorithms to identify profitable patterns in your trading data and incorporate these insights into your performance analysis and strategy refinement.

- Statistical Hypothesis Testing: Employ statistical tests to evaluate the significance of your performance results and avoid drawing misleading conclusions.

Remember, these advanced techniques require a strong foundation in performance analysis fundamentals and a thorough understanding of their potential limitations. Start by mastering the core metrics and gradually progress towards these advanced approaches.

# Chapter Fourteen

## Beyond the Book – Live Trading & Beyond: Diving into the Real World

Congratulations! You've mastered the theoretical foundations of Forex trading and built your first strategy using Python. Now, the real test begins: transitioning from the haven of simulations to the dynamic battlefield of live trading. This chapter equips you with the knowledge and tools to confidently navigate this exciting yet challenging new environment.

## From Sandbox to Real World: Putting Your Skills to the Test

Implementing Limit & Stop Orders: Ditch the simulated environment and execute your trades using real-world orders:

- Master Limit Orders: Define exact price thresholds for entrance and exit, assuring execution at your desired levels or better.
- Harness Stop-Loss Orders: Protect your capital by automatically losing investments, decreasing possible losses.
- Explore Advanced Orders: Utilize Take-Profit orders to lock in gains and Trailing Stop-Loss orders to dynamically adjust exit points based on favorable price movements.

## Calculating Trades & Implementing Strategies

## Apply your theoretical understanding to actual markets:

- Position Sizing: Calculate optimal trade sizes depending on your account balance, risk tolerance, and specified leverage.
- Real-Time Analysis: Monitor live market data and technical indicators, changing your approach depending on shifting market circumstances.
- Emotionless Execution: Stick to your set rules and trading strategy, avoiding hasty judgments caused by fear or greed.
- Beyond Trend-Following: Expanding Your Arsenal

While Trend-Following gives a firm base, investigating additional tactics enables variety and adaptability:

- Mean Reversion: Exploit transient departures from an asset's average price by purchasing inexpensive assets and selling overpriced ones.
- Momentum: Ride strong price swings in either direction by purchasing assets with growing momentum and selling those with diminishing momentum.
- Technical Overlays: Combine various technical indicators like RSI and Bollinger Bands to uncover high-probability trading opportunities.

Remember, every plan has its strengths and drawbacks. Research extensively, backtest exhaustively, and find techniques that correspond with your risk tolerance and trading style.

## Navigating the Live Trading Landscape: The Real Challenges

Live trading includes more than simply strategy and execution. Be prepared for real-world challenges:

- Emotional Trading: Manage fear and greed by keeping to your trading strategy and avoiding hasty actions.
- Slippage: Understand the difference between stated and executed prices, possibly altering your entry and exit points.

- News & Events: Stay updated about economic news and worldwide events that might affect market movements.
- Brokerage Fees & Spreads: Factor in trading charges connected with your selected broker to correctly determine your net returns.

Knowledge is power. By identifying these hurdles and implementing effective risk management strategies, you negotiate the complexity of live trading with more confidence.

## Optimizing Strategies - A Blessing & a Curse

**Striving for improvement is wonderful, but remember:**

- Overfitting: Avoid changing your technique excessively based on insufficient data, since it could perform badly in real-world settings.
- Simplicity vs Complexity: Complex techniques could look "better" in backtests but can be difficult to maintain and prone to overfitting.
- Out-of-Sample Testing: Continuously review your technique on unseen data to guarantee its generalizability and prevent misleading results.

Optimizing your approach is an ongoing effort. Focus on resilience, flexibility, and avoiding the traps of overfitting to guarantee long-term success.

# Closing Thoughts

## The Journey Ahead: Embracing Continuous Learning

Forex trading is a lifelong learning experience. Remember:

- Humility is Key: Accept setbacks as learning experiences and avoid pursuing unrealistic fast riches.
- Continuous Learning: Stay current on market movements, new tactics, and trading psychology to develop your approach.
- Community & Mentorship: Engage with other traders, forums, and mentors to

benefit from their experiences and perspectives.

- Discipline & Patience: Success demands discipline, patience, and smart risk management, not impetuous judgments or pursuing fast rewards.

Embrace the obstacles, consistently learn, and adjust your strategy as you traverse the changing world of Forex trading. Remember, the journey, not just the goal, determines your trading success.

# SHARE YOUR THOUGHTS

Don't just take our word for it! Share your trading journey and help others.

Ready to embark on your own Forex trading adventure? Now that you've equipped yourself with the knowledge and tools from this book, it's time to put theory into practice! Remember, the market awaits, and the journey to your trading goals begins now.

But before you dive in, take a moment to share your experience with this book. Your honest feedback helps us improve and empower future traders like yourself. Leave a positive review on your preferred platform and tell us:

- What resonated most with you?

- How did this book impact your understanding of Forex trading?
- What are your key takeaways and lessons learned?

Your review, both positive and constructive, can be a valuable resource for aspiring traders on the fence. Let's build a community of informed and empowered individuals who navigate the exciting world of Forex with confidence.

Plus, as a small token of appreciation for your review, we'll offer you exclusive access to…

- Exclusive community access: Join a private forum to connect with other readers, ask questions, and share your progress.

- Early access to future content: Be the first to know about upcoming books, courses, or other learning materials.

Leave your review, share your journey, and become part of the Forex trading community! Don't wait, your experience can empower others!

www.ingramcontent.com/pod-product-compliance
Lightning Source LLC
Chambersburg PA
CBHW071047290526
45795CB00004B/1365